When You Pray

by

Daimian R. Edwards

CONTENTS

I was inspired by the Holy Spirit of God to write to all men on how to come to God in prayer. This teaching that Jesus mentioned in **Matthew 6:5-14** is a display of communication between God and man. You must understand that you have to be a believer in Christ for your prayers to have any ef-fect. A believer in Christ loves everything that God loves and hates everything that God hates. God loves people but hates sin.

God's Love for People and Hate towards Sin

Ezekiel 18:23 Do you think that I like to see wicked people die? Says the *Sovereign Lord*. Of course not! I want them to turn from their wicked ways and live. **24** However, if righteous people turn from their righteous behavior and start doing sinful things and act like other sinners, should they be al-lowed to live? No, course not! All their righteous acts will be forgotten, and they will die for their sins. *So, you see God shows no partiality or favoritism for the righteous or the unrighteous meaning the believer or unbe-liever, but His law is just for all."*

What is Sin?

Sin is an <u>immoral act</u> considered to be a <u>transgres-sion</u> against <u>divine law</u>. What's an *immoral act* ? **Im-moral act** applies to one who acts contrary to or does not obey or conform to standards of morality. What is *morality*? **Morality** is principles concerning the distinction between right and wrong or good and bad behavior. What is a *transgression*? **Trans-gression** is an act that goes against a law, rule or code of conduct like, crime, sin, wrongdoing, felony, law-breaking etc.

Last and not least what is *divine law*? **Divine Law** is any law that is understood as obtained from a supreme or superior source or origin, such as the will of God, in contrast to man-made law - meaning Gods law is above every law.

Sin is the reason why Jesus was sent into this world to recon-cile men unto God and to deliver us from Gods wrath upon mankind.

Jesus Came to Deliver Us from Sin

John 3:16 For God loved the world so much that he gave his one and only Son, so that everyone who believes in him will not perish but have eternal life. **17** God sent his Son into the world not to judge the world, but to save the world through him. **18** There is no judgement against anyone who believes in him. But anyone who does not believe in him has already been judged for not believing in God's one and only Son. **19** And the judgement is based on this fact: God's light came into the world, but peo-ple loved the darkness more than the light, for their actions were evil. **20** All who do evil hate the light and refuse to go near it for fear their **sins** will be exposed. **21** But those who do what is right come to the light so others can see that they are doing what God wants. *The conclusion of the matter is this, in order to have effective prayer or communication with God, we must first understand this truth that reconciliation to God the Fa-ther is necessary through Jesus Christ his Son, and also the practice of sin in our lives hinders our prayers.*

John 9:31 Now we know that God heareth not sin-ners: but if any man be a worshipper of God and doeth his will, him he heareth.

3 Things You Must Do

Romans 10:16 But not everyone welcomes the Good News, for Isaiah the prophet said, "LORD, who has believed our message? **17** So faith comes from hearing, that is, hearing the Good News about Christ.

In order for God to hear your prayers, there are three things you must do.

- You must **first** understand and believe that the word of God is true (*the bible*) and is inspired by God. That is called faith.
- **Hebrews 11:1** Now faith is the substance of things hoped for, the evidence of things not seen. Example: You may not be able to see God, but trust His every word.

The 2nd thing you must do according to scripture as the bible states: *Romans 10:9* If you openly de-clare that Jesus is Lord and believe in your heart that God raised him from the dead, you will be saved. *10* For it is by believing in your heart that you are made right with God, and it is by openly declaring your faith that you are saved. **11** As the Scriptures tell us, "Anyone who trusts in him will never be *ashamed* or guilty because of one's actions.

Explained

What does it mean above in verse **9** to declare Jesus as Lord? *To publicly announce Jesus as King or ruler over your life and trusting and obeying his entire word making it law in your heart.*

What are we *saved* from as stated in verses **9-10**? The bible talks about the *wrath* or anger of God, which is the divine punishment for an offense or a *crime* against God according to the scriptures below.

Romans 1:18 "For the wrath of God is revealed from heaven against all ungodliness and unrigh-teousness of men, who by their unrighteousness suppress the truth."

John 3:36 "Whoever believes in the Son has eternal life; whoever does not obey the Son shall not see life, but the wrath of God remains on him."

What is humanities crime against God? In **Genesis Chapter 3,** it talks about the fall of man and how Adam and his wife Eve disobeyed God by eating fruit from a specific tree called (The Tree of Knowledge of Good and Evil). This sin brought a curse upon the earth and future generations that are offsprings of Adam and Eve, according to **Genesis 3:14-19**, but by the grace of God, Jesus was sent from heaven to save us from the wrath of God.

- **I Corinthians 15:21-28, 21** *For since death came through a man, the resurrection of the dead comes also through a man. 22 For as in Adam all die, so in Christ all will be made alive. 23 But each in turn: Christ, the first fruits; then, when he comes, those who belong to him. 24 Then the end will come, when he hands over the kingdom to God the Father after he has destroyed all dominion, authority and power. 25 For he must reign until he has put all his enemies under his feet. 26 The last enemy to be destroyed is death. 27 For he "has put everything under his feet." Now when it says that "everything" has been put under him, it is clear that this does not include God himself, who put everything under Christ. 28 When he has done this, then the Son himself will be made subject to him who put everything under him, so that God may be all in all.*

- **I Thessalonians 5:9** *For God did not appoint us to suffer wrath but to receive salvation through our Lord Jesus Christ.*

The 3rd thing you must do as a believer or new be-liever in Christ is STOP actively following a specific way of life of sin.

- **Leviticus 11:44** I am the Lord your God; <u>consecrate yourselves</u> and be <u>holy</u>, because I am <u>holy</u>. Do not make yourselves unclean by any creature that moves along the ground. **45** I am the Lord, who brought you up out of Egypt to be your God; therefore be <u>holy</u>, because I am <u>holy</u>.

- **1 Peter 1:15** But, as he which hath called you is <u>holy</u>, so be ye holy in manner of conversation **16** for it is written: "Be <u>holy</u>, because I am <u>holy</u>.)"

What does it mean to consecrate yourselves: To dedicate yourself to the service of a deity.

What is a deity: God: Supreme Being or highest in the rank of authority.

What does it mean to be holy: You must be de-voted to the service of God.

What does it mean to be devoted: To be loyal.

What does it mean to be loyal: Faithful to any leader, party or cause.

What does it mean to be faithful: Strict or thor-ough in the performance of duty.

What does the word duty mean: An assigned task, occupation, or place of service.

What does <u>service</u> mean: an act of helpful activ-ity.

What does activity mean: A use of energy or force.

So, we learned above in detail, the full understanding of what it means to be holy as God is holy. As stated above we must first consecrate ourselves, be devoted, loyal, faithful and active in all our duties assigned by God the instant we decide to make Jesus Lord and God over our lives.

Sins That Will Hinder Your Prayers

Galatians 5:19 The acts of the flesh are obvious, *Adultery, fornication, uncleanness, lasciviousness* **20** *idola-try, witchcraft; hatred, variance, emulations, wrath, strife, seditions, heresies* **21** *Envyings, murders, drunkeness, revel-lings* and such like. I warn you, as I did before, that those who live like this will not inherit the kingdom of God.

What is adultery? Voluntary sex between a mar-ried person and a person who is not his or her spouse.

What is fornication? Sex between people who are not married to each other.

What is uncleanness? Morally wrong (unclean, dirty thoughts)

What is lasciviousness? Feeling or revealing an offensive sexual desire openly to someone.

What is Idolatry? The worship of idols: extreme love for something or someone other than God.

What is witchcraft? The practice of sorcery, black magic, the use of spells and acts of calling upon spirits other than God.

What is hatred? Intense or strong dislike.

What is variance? Having heated arguments or disagreements

What are emulations? <u>Dissensions</u>- disagreement that leads to <u>discord</u>- disagreement between two people.

What is wrath? Extreme anger

What is strife? <u>Conflict</u> – a serious disagreement or argument

What are seditions? Trouble making or violent strife.

What are heresies? Belief or opinion entirely dif-ferent from established or approved religious (espe-cially Christian) doctrine

What are envyings? The desire for oneself (some-thing possessed or enjoyed by another)

What does it mean to murder? Unlawful premed- itated killing of one human being by another

What is drunkenness? The state of being <u>intoxi- cated</u> - alcoholic drink or a drug causing someone to lose control of their physical power or behavior

What is revellings? To be <u>disorderly</u> - involving or contributing to a breakdown of peaceful and law-abiding behavior

Rightful Living = Prayers Not Hindered

Galatians 5:22 But the fruit of the Spirit is *love, joy, peace, longsuffering, gentleness, goodness, faith,* **23** *meekness and temperance.* Against such things there is no law. **24** Those who belong to Christ Jesus have crucified the flesh with its passions and desires. **25** Since we live by the Spirit, let us keep in step with the Spirit. **26** Let us not become *conceited, provoking* and *envying* each other.

What is the fruit of the Spirit? The fruit of the Holy Spirit is a biblical term that sums up nine characteristics of a person or community living in accord with the Holy Spirit.

What is love? An intense feeling of deep affection.

What is joy? A feeling of great pleasure and happi-ness.

What is peace? <u>Kindness</u> - the quality of being friendly, generous, and considerate.

What is longsuffering? Having or showing pa-tience in spite of troubles caused by other people.

What is gentleness? The quality of being kind, tender, or mild-mannered.

What is goodness? The quality of being morally good or honest.

What is faith? Complete trust or confidence in someone or something.

What is meekness? <u>Submissiveness</u> – The quality of being ready to conform to the authority or will of others.

What is temperance? Abstinence - the fact or practice of restraining oneself from indulging in something, typically alcohol.

What is conceited? Excessively proud of oneself.

What is provoking? Causing annoyance; irritating.

What is envying? Desire to have a quality, posses-sion, or other desirable attribute belonging to some-one else.

Now' that we have explained everything
above, let us learn how to pray!

Jesus Instructions on Prayer

Matthew 6:5 When you pray don't be like the hyp-ocrites who love to pray publicly on street corners and in the synagogues where everyone can see them. I tell you the truth, that is all the reward they will ever get. **6** But *when you pray*, go away by your-self, shut the door behind you, and pray to your Fa-ther in private. Then your Father, who sees every-thing, will reward you. **7** *When you pray*, don't babble on and on as people of other religions do. They think their prayers are answered merely by repeat-ing their words again and again. **8** Don't be like them, for your Father knows exactly what you need even before you ask him!

Explained!

Vs. 5 <u>Don't be like the hypocrites</u> - means a person who indulges in hypocrisy.

Indulge – means to satisfy one's desires and feel-ings.

Hypocrisy – having some desirable or publicly ap-proved attitude or virtuous character, moral or reli-gious beliefs or principles that one does not pos-sess. *In other words, to put on an act for public approval.*

Vs. 6 *Don't pray to be seen or to please others publicly in-stead be sincere when you pray* - God is not saying that you shouldn't pray publicly, but when you do pray, make sure it is from the heart, and God will reward you for being sincere.

Vs. 7 *Don't be like other religions using vain repetitions.* In other words, don't keep repeating yourself over and over again while praying to God. Prayer is a two-way conversation. Talk to God and wait for a re-sponse having faith that he will answer you in due time. God might not answer you the same day, but keep seeking Him day to day until he answers you.

Vs. 8 He knows your needs before you ask Him. *He Knows* - means he has knowledge

Your Needs – something required that is very impor-tant

Verses 9-14

Jesus states: **9** After this manner therefore pray ye: Our Father which art in heaven, Hallowed be thy name. **10** Thy kingdom come. Thy will be done in earth, as it is in heaven. **11** Give us this day our daily bread **12** And forgive us our debts, as we forgive our debtors. 13 And lead us not into temptation, but deliver us from evil: For thine is the kingdom and the power, and the glory, forever. Amen. **14**

For if ye forgive men their trespasses, your heav-enly Father will also forgive you **15** But if ye forgive not men their trespasses, neither will your Father forgive your trespasses.

Explained

Vs. 9 Jesus is instructing us how to come to His Fa-ther which is now our Father. *Pray like this* [In other words, don't do anything different than what I am telling you.

Our Father - The word *our* means belonging to or associated with.

Father – means – A man in relation (an existing con-nection) to his natural child or children.

Hallowed be your name- means – May your name be kept Holy - *Holy* means – to honor as holy, conse-crated, sanctified - set apart.

Name means – Is Known or referred too.

Vs. 10 *Thy Kingdom come* - We desire for Christ to es-tablish His kingdom soon.

Thy will be done – *will* means expressing the future tense. In other words, Jesus is saying that we should pray that the way things are done in heaven should be the same way things are done on earth. Jesus prays this to His father in reference to His *will, three* times in the garden of Gethsemane. Matthew: 26:36-4

Vs. 11 *Give us this day our daily bread means* - Give us what we need daily.

Vs. 12 And forgive us our debts, as we forgive our debtors. *Forgive*- stop feeling angry or resentful toward someone for an offense, flaw or mistake.

Debts - something that is owed. God gave us this earth, and we squandered it in the Garden of Eden (Genesis chapter 3) when mankind sinned against Him. God sent Jesus to repay what was lost, and we owe Him our loyalty for giving us eternal life. Our payback is to love God and to love others.

Vs. 13 *And lead us not into temptation* . [Don't let us yield or surrender to the desire to do something wrong or unwise] but deliver us from evil or [the evil one which is Satan]

Vs. 14 If you forgive those who sin against you, your heavenly Father will forgive you.
Vs. 15 But if you refuse to forgive others, your Father will not forgive your sins.

Jesus repeats 3 times about forgiveness in vs. 12 - 15. Why? Unforgiveness is in the same category as sin, and we know how God feels about sin already, don't we? Don't forget sin hinders prayers.

Conclusion

The bottom line is this. Practicing sin and having an unforgiving heart will hinder your prayers. Most importantly, we must understand how to approach God in prayer, which we have just learned from our King Jesus! If you have understood all that you have read and would like to invite Jesus into your heart please repeat this prayer of salvation on the next page!

Prayer of Salvation

Father God, I have read and understood all that was written in this book and came to realize in my heart that I need a Savior. King Jesus, Lord and God of the universe, I denounce the kingdom of Satan from my life and now give my whole heart, mind, soul, spirit and body totally over to you. Lord' Jesus, I trust you to keep your every word and that the bible is true. Father, thank you for giving me a new life in your Son Jesus, and by the power of your Holy Spirit, I am now a new creature and made righteous in your site. In Jesus Mighty Name I Pray! Amen!

I hope this helps you on your journey in your prayer life. One love in Christ Jesus to all men, women and children around the world. God Bless!

Written by: Daimian R. Edwards
Inspired by the Holy Spirit!

About the Author

Daimian R. Edwards has been a devoted born-again Christian since the age of 17. He has been married to his wife of 21 years, has three children and resides in New Jersey. His main desire through his lifetime is reaching people through the gospel of Jesus Christ. Now, in his early 40's he has been inspired by the Spirit of God to write and tell the world about what he has learned over the years and to turn humanity's focus on building a relationship with Jesus Christ the Savior of the world.

Please visit our website and join our email list for future projects alerts!

Website: www.daimiane.com

Editor: Lisa Thornton Stillwell & Arkonna

Cover Art: Kozakura / Clip Art Image

Scripture Translations for this book: NIV, KJV,AMP, NKJV